WEIGHT LOSS - A SUSTAINABLE APPROACH

LOSE EXCESS FAT THIS VEGAN WAY AND SLEEP LIKE A BABY

PRADEEP KUMAR PANDEY

ISBN 979-888503342-8

Contents

A Few Lines About This Book

Are you someone looking for an effective, flexible, and sustainable fat loss plan? A plan that hits excess body fat with multiple strategies incorporated into one clear-cut package so that we can shed those extra kilos more constructively and keep them off for the rest of our life?

And do you also want to improve your sleep quality and follow a healthy lifestyle?

Then, I believe this book could be of substantive help to you!

I have come up with a plan that is a mix of whatever I have learned in the past few years of my life. I have applied it and seen the results in reduced excess fat, with much-improved sleep without using any supplements. The plan also increases mental focus, clarity of thought, enhanced decision making, and alertness throughout the day.

I have also increased my insulin sensitivity and reduced the ill effects of night-shift work by just changing how, what, and when I eat and sleep according to my work schedule. In addition, I have minimized my prolonged sitting-related lower back pain, reduced stress, increased my productivity at work, and improved my eyesight as a result of following this plan for a few years.

Now I have room for whatever I want to eat that makes me feel good while still losing any stubborn belly fat. And, more importantly, I feel great, have sustained energy throughout the day, and am strongly motivated to continue with this program for the rest of my life.

I want to spread these ideas and the practical, sustainable strategy throughout this book to a wide audience.

The book aims to explain this tried-and-tested strategy that can do wonders for someone looking for a sustainable, easy-to-manage, and flexible fat loss plan.

Disclaimer

Weight Loss—A Sustainable Approach
Lose excess fat this vegan way and sleep like a baby
By:
PRADEEP KUMAR PANDEY
Diploma (Health, Nutrition and Weight loss)
Bachelor of Engineering (Computer Science)
DISCLAIMER

The information and ideas discussed in this book result from what I have observed and gained through studying modern health-related concerns and effective ways to address them in order to reduce or minimize them and attain general well-being. The author has applied these strategies in his own life and has found them helpful. They are for educational purposes only and do not substitute for professional medical, health, or personal advice.

Readers are always requested to seek the guidance of their doctor or other qualified health professional if they have any questions about their health or a medical condition before trying any of the methods or ideas illustrated in this book. The author will not be responsible for any health-related concerns arising or worsening after following his advice. He expects readers to do their research before applying the strategies discussed in this book.

CHAPTER I

High-Quality Sleep and its Importance

Sleep is the first step towards achieving general good health and well-being, even if you are not trying to lose fat. Having a good night's sleep and feeling refreshed on waking can have wonderful effects that we are not even aware of. Sleeping well can:

- reduce stress, overall fat build-up, and cravings for food, especially unhealthy food;
- increase alertness, focus, and productivity (and improve decision making) throughout the following day;
- boost feelings of happiness and confidence, improve mood, and reduce irritability; and
- promote hormonal balance in the body.

One study from the Sleep Research Society found that people with reduced sleep duration had a much higher likelihood of becoming obese.[1]We also make poor food choices, taking in more calories than required when our sleep–wake cycle is inadequate. Insufficient sleep can result in depression in people of all ages, and vice versa.[2]It can also contribute to ongoing lower back pain, and decrease our mental focus and productivity.[3]

Short-term consequences of sleep disruption include heightened stress responsivity; reduced quality of life; emotional distress; mood disorders; cognition, memory, and performance issues; and behavior problems in otherwise healthy individuals.

Long-term consequences of sleep disruption include hypertension, dyslipidemia, weight-related issues, metabolic syndrome, and Type 2 diabetes. Evidence suggests that sleep disruption may increase the risk of certain cancers and death. Chronic sleep disruption may also worsen some gastrointestinal disorders.

According to the Centers for Disease Control and Prevention, an adult aged between 18 and 60 should aim for 7 or more hours of sleep a night.[4]This can vary depending on certain factors like the kinds of activity we do in our day, the hormonal changes in our body, and our diet and lifestyle factors. We should find out the appropriate amount of sleep required to carry out our daily activities comfortably, generally ranging from 6 to 9 hours.

If, most of the time, we wake up feeling refreshed each morning without any alarm, that's a good sign that we are getting enough sleep. If we do not get daytime drowsiness that often (except after large meals), this means that we are getting a good amount of sleep in the night. If our productivity does not suffer due to lack of sleep, this suggests that we are sleeping adequately.

But suppose that we do not get enough sleep one day for whatever reason. In this case, we should try to lessen the impact of this by taking a few short 20-minute naps during the rest of the day, preferably in the afternoon, or try to cover the sleep debt the next day by sleeping some extra hours: combining today's quota and yesterday's missing quota. So, if 7 hours' sleep was what we aimed to achieve and we could achieve only 5 hours on a given night, then the next day we must strive to sleep for 7+2 (backlog) = 9 hours to make up for it.

As with everything, more is not always best: more sleep than required by the body can lead to insomnia. This is because, if we take huge naps in the afternoon (say, 2–3 hours, then this will disrupt our normal nighttime sleep and we will not get enough timely sleep during the night. However, sleeping for extended hours can be helpful occasionally, especially if, for example, we are sick, feeling weak or in pain, or need to compensate for a hectic weeklong schedule. It depends. But, if we do this more often, our sleep on weekdays will also be affected because we are altering our sleep–wake cycle to sleep longer than usual but only sparingly and as needed.

I avoid taking naps in the day because it disrupts my sleep–wake cycle and I feel sleepy the next day, usually around the time of my nap the previous day. Instead, I have my daily quota of required sleep and prepare myself to make up for any lack of sleep by walking more in my break time every hour and drinking more water each day. I also eat some snacks, and watch short video clips about investing and trading strategies to make my mind think or calculate. I also find watching some short comedy shows helpful in getting me through the day.

This is just a workaround, however, to fix my productivity-related issues to some extent. That's why we must have a perfect sleep–wake schedule that helps us sleep like a baby. Interestingly enough, on this program, I save time in falling asleep after going to bed and wake up feeling refreshed a little earlier, thereby saving time at both ends, which I can then put towards extra work.

Dr Robert Stickgold pointed out a study that suggested a link between sleep loss and increased impairment in judgment.[5]

The Institute of Medicine estimates that drowsy driving is responsible for roughly 20% of all kinds of motor vehicle crashes. This means that such driving causes approximately

1 million crashes, 500,000 injuries, and 8,000 deaths each year in the United States.[6]

I try to keep my sleep–wake schedule fixed. I go to bed at the same time every day and wake up most days almost automatically before my alarm goes off. This is very, very important! My body gets accustomed to this schedule and prepares itself in advance to perform its daily operations when I send strong signals to my brain—by going into the daylight as soon as possible upon waking up—that my day has started. I stay in the sunlight for at least 15 to 30 minutes to let my body set the stage for the rest of the day by increasing melatonin in the evening, an important hormone responsible for sleep.

However, what is most critical is to get up at or around the same time every day when we can arrange this, although going to bed at a specified time every day may not be feasible for some people. Every day is different and, sometimes, we are unable to go to sleep on time for whatever reason.

If falling asleep becomes difficult, performing some bedtime rituals helps prepare us for sleep, including reading books in which we can immerse ourselves, thereby reducing our stress level and calming our mind. However, it depends upon what we are reading. We must find out what kind of content brings us calm and relief from the day's stress, and use it daily so that our body knows that we are about to sleep.

However, I will now discuss the next crucial step, which will lead us to sleep like babies even when we do not follow any bedtime ritual.

Despite lack of deep sleep, my highest work performance was achieved due to workarounds when I had no access to such knowledge and didn't know what to do.

I did not seek any professional medical help because I did not want to take any medication for insomnia.. Instead, I just listened to my own experience and tried the following to increase my productivity.

1. I fixed my sleeping and waking up times and slept (or rested, I should say, because I did not feel like sleeping). I switched off my mobile, closed my eyes, and stayed in bed for 10 to 12 hours at a stretch because I had to work a shift after waking up. I was having significant issues with my sleep quality.

2. I did not check my social media profiles for the entire 15 days when had I decided to get the work done at any cost, despite my sleep disorder. This strategy helped me focus on the job and provided mental calmness while resting in bed.

3. I set a half-hourly to hourly target and a deadline to finish a particular piece of work, writing these down and monitoring them every hour or so.

4. I took frequent breaks after completing my hourly targets and walked around for 2 to 5 minutes in these breaks. I drank more water, took some fresh air outside, then came back, set another target and deadline for the next hour, and repeated until the shift end, which also helped me reduce my prolonged sitting-related lower back pain to some extent.

5. Because I had increased my focus on my work, my body and brain were wired in a way like never before and I did not feel much of the lower back pain when doing the shift work.

As a result, I finished doing—in just 15 days—an amount of work that would usually take me 30 days to do!

So I felt like sharing this information with anyone who wanted to increase their productivity, even when they could not sleep well, by getting started with this program.

If you have any level of sleep disorder or insomnia, first try the following:

1. Fixing your daily sleep and waking up time—most importantly, the waking up time.

2. Going out into bright daylight every day at around the same time, and staying there for at least 30 minutes to an hour.

3. Sticking to this routine throughout your life as much as possible.

When we don't follow a consistent sleep–wake routine, our body and brain get confused as to when to prepare for sleeping and waking. So this needs to be fixed.

In a matter of just a week or two, we can see significant improvement in our sleep when following this method.

I have tried taking over-the-counter melatonin supplements for sleep (3–10 mg), starting with 3 mg, then increasing to 10 mg. This helped in terms of sound quality sleep daily but, after a couple of months, my body stopped responding to it. I even tried taking 20–30 mg of melatonin daily one hour before bedtime, but this did not help me go to sleep in time and it increased my daytime drowsiness when I was supposed to be working. That's why I'm not going to recommend that you take any melatonin supplements for sleep.

Natural melatonin boosters like tart cherries, walnuts, and rice did not provide many benefits either. Later on, I became aware of an essential factor that assured high-quality sleep without using any of these. I will discuss this in Chapter 2.

It is a good idea to keep a log of our sleep timings and duration, how we feel after waking up, and the effects of these on our day, so that we can tweak the hours and timings that suit us best and will be the most fruitful. These vary from person to person.

Some points to consider for good sleep:

1. Taking a last meal or snack, preferably 3 to 4 hours before bedtime, is beneficial, as supported by the following quote from a *Times of India* (TOI) article[7]:

The ideal time gap between dinner and breakfast:

Our digestive system takes 3 to 4 hours to digest the food completely. So, the ideal gap between your breakfast-lunch and lunch-dinner should not be more than 4 hours. Exceeding the time limit may cause acidity in the stomach. But when we talk about the gap between dinner and breakfast, it is advised to stick to a 12–14 hours fasting. Exceeding this time limit is also not considered suitable for your weight loss journey. By sticking to this specific time window, you will lose weight effectively and are less likely to develop cardiovascular problems. Fasting for a minimum of 12 hours between your dinner and breakfast is excellent for the complete digestion of food. It will also promote sound sleep and help to maintain the cardinal rhythm of the body.

2. Keeping a gap of a minimum of 2 hours between taking our last meal and lying down on our bed before sleep is essential.

3. Getting our body into a fat-burning zone before or around bedtime seems to be necessary so that our brain can carry out its tasks more efficiently. I keep, for example, a 6–8-hour gap between the last meal of the day and sleep. This has helped me to get more high-quality sleep, and to feel pleasant and refreshed on waking up. We can each adjust to what works best for us.

4. Avoiding alcohol consumption before bedtime helps with sleep.

5. Reading a book in which we can become immersed reduces stress levels and lowers cortisol significantly, thereby promoting good sleep.

6. Sleeping in a coolish room helps with sleep quality. We may wake up in the middle of the night if the room temperature is not so cool, especially in the summer. We can always find out what temperature is best for us in helping us sleep: usually 21–22 degrees Celsius.

7. Sleeping on a suitable mattress may also improve our sleep.

Maximum fat loss happens when we sleep, especially if we eat early in the evening long before bedtime: this gives our body an excellent window in which to burn that excess fat that most of us are carrying around.

I don't want to promote this method by showing you weight loss data in a specified period. Everybody is different and should never compare their weight loss achievement to anyone else's. I just wanted to share an idea of what I have found to be the most effective strategy to lose excess weight.

My wife lost 5 kg (11 pounds) in just 3 weeks on this program. However, that doesn't mean that I also lost in the same ratio!

[1]https://bmcpublichealth.biomedcentral.com/articles/10.1186/s12889-016-2913-4

[2]https://www.sciencedirect.com/science/article/pii/S0950329320303438

[3]https://www.spine-health.com/wellness/sleep/chronic-pain-and-insomnia-breaking-cycle

[4]https://www.cdc.gov/sleep/about_sleep/how_much_sleep.html

[5]https://healthysleep.med.harvard.edu/healthy/matters/benefits-of-sleep/learning-memory

[6]https://healthysleep.med.harvard.edu/need-sleep/whats-in-it-for-you/judgment-safety

[7]'Weight loss: The NO-COMPROMISE time gap between your dinner and breakfast,' *The Times of India* (May 27, 2019). https://timesofindia.indiatimes.com/life-style/health-fitness/weight-loss/weight-loss-the-no-compromise-time-gap-between-your-dinner-and-breakfast/articleshow/69483862.cms

CHAPTER II

Circadian Rhythm

"Exercising during both early morning and late afternoon can boost circadian rhythm. Our ancestors were active throughout their day, but especially in the morning and evening.
—Dr Satchin Panda "

We can get the highest quality sleep by keeping our sleep–wake cycles tuned to our circadian rhythm.

Living in alignment with our circadian rhythms—like our ancestors did back in the days when there was no electricity, light bulbs, or Internet—can do wonders for our overall health and well-being.

Our Wonderful Circadian Rhythm

Unfortunately, we don't know much about our circadian rhythm, although it plays an essential role in regulating our sleep–wake cycle. Our body has an internal clock that keeps ticking. On waking up, if we go out into bright daylight, a certain amount and intensity of light perceived by our eyes set up our internal body clock for the rest of the day. The light triggers specific chemical reactions that a) tell our body and brain that this is daytime, and b) send strong signals to start their operations for our sleeping time by increasing melatonin in the evening to prepare us for sleep.

We must aim for between 15 minutes' and 2 hours' exposure to bright daylight, depending on how bad our sleep has been affected by not doing so—that is, having much-reduced exposure to bright sunlight when we get up. In these modern days, due to electric bulbs and screens, we are constantly exposed to blue light in the evening and night. This disrupts our internal clock, leading to various kinds of sleep disorders.

Spending time outdoors during the day also increases the 'happy hormone', serotonin, which has a positive role on mental health by reducing depression, anxiety, etc. When we expose ourselves to brighter daylight after waking up, this reduces the impact of the blue light that we are exposed to in the latter part of the day. It helps us to feel sleepy just at the right time and also to get up the next day feeling refreshed—most of the time at least.

So here are some suggestions for actions to take if you are unable to get enough sleep at night:

1. Set a fixed sleeping and waking schedule.

2. Get up at the same time every day, go into bright daylight on waking up, and stay there for at least 30 minutes. Being in this bright light for up to 2 hours while walking, observing the nature around us, feeling the fresh air, and taking some slow deep breaths are all suggested if we want to improve our sleep quality and duration quickly, and have time to do so. However, do not expose yourself to too much sunlight because it can cause severe damage. Please refer to Chapter 10 for more information on getting vitamin D from sunlight correctly if you stay in very bright sunny days for periods of more than 2 hours.

3. I recommend dimming the lights and reducing the blue light exposure 1–2 hours before you plan to go to bed so that your body gets the idea that it is evening time now

and it can start releasing melatonin to prepare you for sleep. It is also good to wear orange or red glasses to minimize the effects of blue light if we do not dim the lights 1 hour before bedtime.

4. I use an app called 'Lux' on my mobile. This tells me whether the amount of light in my room will help me sleep or not. I work night shifts so some daylight is unavoidable in the daytime. The ideal lux number for promoting sleep is around 10. We can also check the amount of lux we have in the day when we wake up, as well as our blue light bulbs and screen lux levels in the evening. If we cannot wake up before evening or live in an area where proper sunlight is not available during the daytime, we can use some light therapy boxes. Even a cloudy day is much brighter than our light bulbs at night, so it will also help if we stay in this light for a reasonable amount of time before going back to our usual blue light. People who can't get proper daylight exposure for some reason may use light therapy boxes. Exposure to a 10,000 lux light therapy bulb for 30 minutes a day is said to be healthy. It works best when we face it from a distance of about 24 inches. However, it depends on what type of light therapy box it is and from which company.

5. It is also helpful to perform a bedtime ritual, like reading a book or listening to a constant pattern of noise, such as the sounds of falling rain or bells, which we can practice listening to daily close to our bedtime. I practice meditation by lying down, taking slow deep breaths through the nose and exhaling by mouth, trying to concentrate on my breath, breaking my chain of thoughts, if any, with eyes closed, until I fall asleep.

6. Not eating close to bedtime is very helpful for quality sleep. It can vary according to one's schedule and what's feasible. I have my last meal 7 hours before my sleep time

because this puts my body into the fat-burning zone before sleeping so that I can sleep tight. This may not be necessary for everybody though. Taking our last meal 4 hours before sleep can also do the job. But one should avoid eating close to bedtime because it can disrupt our sleep.

If you have not already done so, you may like to refer to an informative book by Dr Satchin Panda (*The Circadian Code*)[1]for much more detailed information on the internal clock and the importance of time-restricted eating. I recommend this if you work a night shift or experience jet lag.

Whenever, for whatever reason, I'm unable to get exposure to bright daylight on getting up so that I'm feeling sleepy when starting my work, I try some work-around. I stand closer to the room's 20-watt LED bulb, facing it from about 1 foot or so, and check the lux, which should be around 9,000. Then, I face this bright light for about 20 minutes or so and, after this bright light exposure, my sleepiness has gone. I no longer feel sleepy after this bright light exposure.[2]

I suggest that those who experience periodic jet lag, due to traveling to different time zones across the world, carry portable light therapy boxes to tune their circadian rhythm according to their working hours or shift timings.

[1]https://www.amazon.in/Circadian-Code-weight-supercharge-energy/dp/1785042017

[2]Note, though, that exposing oneself to strong bright light for a much longer time can result in mania episodes, so one should try it with caution.

CHAPTER III

Managing Insulin Spikes

This chapter discusses the required macronutrient formula to trigger desired fat loss and decrease insulin spikes, why it may be responsible for modern diet and lifestyle-related diseases, and how to manage it.

Studies have shown that fat deposition or lipogenesis Is stimulated by insulin, an anabolic hormone. The conventional 3-meals-a-day schedule with sporadic snacking causes random blood glucose and insulin surges throughout the day.[1]

Fat build-up is determined by the balance between lipogenesis and lipolysis/fatty acid oxidation. In the past few years, our understanding of the nutritional, hormonal, and particularly transcriptional regulation of lipogenesis has expanded greatly. Lipogenesis is stimulated by a high carbohydrate diet, whereas it is inhibited by polyunsaturated fatty acids and by fasting. These effects are partly mediated by hormones, which inhibit (growth hormone, leptin) or stimulate (insulin) lipogenesis. Recent research has established that the sterol regulatory element binding protein-1 is a critical intermediate in the pro- or anti-lipogenic action of several hormones and nutrients. Another transcription factor implicated in lipogenesis is the peroxisome proliferator activated receptor γ. Both transcription factors are attractive targets for pharmaceutical intervention of disorders such as hypertriglyceridemia and obesity.[2]

It seems that most of the modern diseases such as obesity, type 2 diabetes, cardiovascular disease, and cancer correlate to hyperinsulinemia—that is, an abnormal increase in insulin in our blood. So we should pay attention to the insulin spikes that occur due to our intake of certain types of food, mainly highly processed simple carbohydrates such as white bread, refined wheat flour, and rice. Intake of lean protein also contributes to insulin spikes.

A recent PubMed Central article published in July 2021 stated that consumption of the 'modern' Western diet and over-nutrition might increase insulin secretion, decrease insulin pulses, and/or reduce hepatic insulin clearance, causing hyperinsulinemia.[3]

Hyperinsulinemia disturbs the balance of the insulin growth hormone (GH)–insulin-like growth factor axis and shifts the insulin:GH ratio towards insulin and away from GH. This insulin-GH shift promotes energy storage and lipid synthesis, and hinders lipid breakdown, resulting in obesity due to higher fat accumulation and lower energy expenditure. Abnormally increased insulin is a critical etiological factor in developing metabolic syndrome, type 2 diabetes, cardiovascular disease, cancer, and premature mortality.

It might also be the case that nutritionally driven insulin exposure controls the rate of mammalian aging. Caloric restriction, increasing hepatic insulin clearance, and maximizing insulin sensitivity are, at present, the three main strategies available for managing hyperinsulinemia. They may slow down age-related physiological decline and prevent age-related diseases.

Your total carbohydrate intake at a meal is the main factor influencing your blood sugar levels. If you want to stabilize your blood sugar levels (reduce insulin spikes), avoid choosing foods that are high in carbohydrates (such as wheat, rice, sugar, and highly processed junk foods), or limit your serving size of high-carb foods.[4]

Thus, it is imperative to eat a meal that does not cause insulin spikes to such an extent. We should minimize or eliminate *simple* carbs as much as possible and replace them with *complex* carbs, some protein, healthy fats (extra-virgin olive oil, cold-pressed coconut oil, cold-pressed/kachi ghani mustard oil), fiber or salads, vegetables, etc.

We should eat a balanced meal or snack—say, complex carbs, protein, healthy fat (mainly obtained from plants; please refer to Chapter 6 for more information on this), salads/fiber and greens. With the reduction of simple carbs, sugar, junk food, and unhealthy oils in our diet, and the addition of more complex carbs, protein, and healthy fats, we can go for extended periods without having our next meal again too soon. This strategy will not cause insulin spikes that much. It will also reduce our total caloric intake in the day, because we will feel full after eating such a combination. The overall caloric deficit leads to fat loss.

This type of meal or snack also significantly reduces our craving for more food too soon, and we stop getting serious hunger pangs with the addition of healthy fats, because the body takes more time to process them.

Even if we follow such a diet and don't get into a caloric deficit by burning more than our caloric intake, the excess calories will get stored as fat. Therefore, the next step is to give the body that fat-burning window so that we don't not have to worry about counting calories and we still lose weight.

Simple carbohydrates are refined flour, white bread, white rice, pastries, sodas, snacks, pasta, sweets, candy, sugary drinks, soda, baked goods, cakes, and fruit juices. It is recommended to minimize such simple carbs from one's diet.

Complex carbs are carbohydrate-rich foods that are difficult to digest and a more stable source of energy than simple carbohydrates.

Healthy fats help regulate blood glucose levels by making the glucose sources digest more slowly, releasing the sugar into the blood over a much more extended period.

Fat slows down the digestion process by delaying gastric emptying, which can help prevent a quick and drastic rise in your blood sugar levels after eating. People with diabetes adding two tablespoons of olive oil to mashed potatoes, a high-glycemic carbohydrate food (known for insulin spikes), kept their blood sugar levels more steady - The Journal of Clinical Endocrinology & Metabolism (2006).

Examples of vegan sources of complex carbohydrates are:

- barley;
- yams;
- hand-pounded rice (unpolished);
- rye;
- potatoes with skin;
- quinoa;
- pumpkin;
- millets (gluten-free grains);
- chickpeas;
- sweet potatoes;
- kamut;
- beans;
- lentils;
- green peas.

Examples of vegan sources of protein are:

- quinoa;
- pulses;
- chickpeas;
- beans;
- tofu;
- nuts and seeds, such as hemp seeds and pumpkin seeds;
- buckwheat; and
- green peas.

Examples of healthy fats for vegans are:

- coconut fruit/coconut oil;
- nuts;
- extra-virgin olive oil;
- cold pressed (kachi ghani) mustard oil;
- avocado;
- cacao nibs.

Eating seasonal fruits and vegetables in some quantity will ensure your required fiber intake.[5]

What you eat with your carbohydrates matters, too. 'Protein and fat slow the absorption of glucose into the bloodstream, which helps prevent [insulin] spikes and drops,' says Jamieson-Petonic.[6]Pairing an apple with peanut butter or serving rice with beans and avocado can lessen the blood-sugar impact of the whole plate. That all might sound pretty complex, but the bottom line is simple: the less processed your food and the more work your body has to do to digest it, the better it is for your blood sugar.[7]

Compared with a white rice-based breakfast, a bean-based diet significantly reduces postprandial glucose levels and promotes insulin secretion. These results support a dietary approach to reducing postprandial hyperglycemia.[8]

That's why it is vital to reduce consumption of simple carbohydrates, such as white rice, and include more complex carbs, such as beans.

When we are more active or when our organs of the body are growing as in earlier parts of our life, insulin spikes are not that much of an issue, because they're just meant to drive growth in our body. Insulin is a hormone that is responsible for allowing glucose in the blood to enter cells to provide them with the energy to function. If our body cannot handle insulin effectively, it can lead to development of diabetes, due to insulin resistance. When we are sedentary/not much physically active, or are fully grown up, we need to be more cautious about our insulin spikes because in addition to increased fat deposition, it may fuel abnormal growths such as certain cancers[9]or tumors inside our body.

I would highly recommend reading books such as 'Why We Get Sick' by Benjamin Bikman, which gives us an in-depth analysis of insulin and insulin resistance and also 'Zero Belly Diet' by David Zinczenko, which shows us more examples of how to combine our food items to get reduced insulin spikes, which leads to fat loss and overall good health.

You can also use Cronometerto check which food has got what type of macronutrients and micronutrients. They also have an app for Android and iOS to access their services on your smartphone.

[1]https://medium.com/beingwell/why-restricting-calories-doesnt-work-eb35e0add77

[2]https://www.ncbi.nlm.nih.gov/pmc/articles/PMC1083868/

[3]https://www.ncbi.nlm.nih.gov/pmc/articles/PMC6817492/

[4]'Food Combinations to Steady Blood Sugar & Raise Metabolism'. https://healthyeating.sfgate.com/food-combinations-steady-blood-sugar-raise-metabolism-1670.html.

[5]If you are allergic to any of the food items mentioned in this book, I suggest that you talk to your physician before trying them out on your own.

[6]https://www.sharecare.com/health/diabetes/article/how-eat-avoid-insulin-spikes

[7]https://www.sharecare.com/health/diabetes/article/how-eat-avoid-insulin-spikes

[8]https://pubmed.ncbi.nlm.nih.gov/33785707/

[9]https://www.ncbi.nlm.nih.gov/pmc/articles/PMC1204764/

CHAPTER IV

Millets

Millet is a cereal grain that we should include in our diet instead of wheat and rice to reduce insulin spikes and ensure good blood sugar management.[1]

Nutritional Value and Health Benefits

Regulating Blood Glucose Levels
Millets have a low glycemic index and are gluten free, high in dietary fiber, proteins, amino acids, vitamins, and minerals. They stabilize blood sugar levels, preventing spikes and promoting insulin sensitivity.

Helping in Weight Loss

With a high percentage of fibrous content, antioxidants, protein, low calories, gluten-free status, and high complex carbohydrates, millets are the ideal food for weight loss. Replacing rice, wheat etc. with millets helps lower your body mass index (BMI), prevents accumulation of fat, improves gut health, and helps you to achieve sustained weight loss.

Improves Heart Health

Millets contain antioxidants that include beta-glucans, tannins, flavonoids, lignans, anthocyanidins, and policosanols. These antioxidants help in lowering low-density lipoprotein (LDL) cholesterol (sometimes called 'bad cholesterol') and in clearing clots and keeping blood vessels healthy. In this way, they lower the risk of heart disease, blood pressure, and stroke.

Preventing the Formation of Cancer Cells

Foxtail and proso varieties of millets have been proved effective in inhibiting the growth of cancerous cells in various tissues.[2]Phytochemicals in millets have an antiproliferative effect and lower formation of cancer cells in the colon, breast, and liver without causing damage to normal cells.

Assisting Digestion

The high dietary fibre in millets helps in improving the digestive function. Millets are alkaline, reducing the risk of gastrointestinal conditions such as gastric ulcers and colon cancers. They help to overcome constipation, excess gas, bloating, and cramping, and regularize bowel function.

Improving Immunity

Millets improve the overall health of other vital organs like the liver and kidneys, and boost the immune system.

People have lost weight, lowered their blood sugar, and maintained their weight after a few months of eating millets instead of wheat or white rice. This simple change in diet leads to a much healthier body over time.

Ever since I started using millets to replace wheat and rice, I noticed that I was no longer bloated after eating them, as I had previously been after eating white bread. My weight did not go up after I ate millets 2–3 times a day for a month. I also had much-reduced heartburn episodes, which had been prominent when I used to eat wheat. My weight would increase every week even if I was only consuming small amounts of roti (chapatti)—say, 2 twice a day—but, with millets, that was not the case. However, I used to get hungry when I ate polished millets, because some millets in their original form are hard to digest on account of their high fiber content.

According to Dr Khader Valli, an Indian scientist and authority on millets, people can get tremendous health benefits from including millets in their diet.[3]

[1]https://medium.com/illumination/millets-the-panacea-for-diabetes-weight-loss-cancers-heart-ailments-and-a-host-of-other-health-5d207917ba47

[2]https://pubmed.ncbi.nlm.nih.gov/26075747

[3]See   https://www.siridhanya.comfor   more information or millet recipes. The website is also an online millets store.

CHAPTER V

Natural Fat Burners

Natural fat burners are foods that trigger fat loss and we must include them in any fat loss program.

The following types of foods have been proven to trigger fat burning.

1. Coffee

Coffee contains caffeine and other compounds that help in the breakdown of fat tissues in our body. It can also boost our metabolism, which can, in turn, increase the rate at which we burn energy, leading to increased caloric expenditure overall.

However, we should monitor our coffee intake and keep it moderate (1–2 cups for best results) so as to not develop tolerance. I take it with three teaspoons of wood-pressed coconut oil and some sugar to give it some taste. No milk, no animal fat. And it gives me a good energy boost and triggers fat burning efficiently (more on coconut oil in section 4 below).

Ashley Richmond writes on Medium:

"Coffee is incredibly healthy. Most people don't think this is true, but it is. It's full of antioxidants, cancer-preventing substances, and it can improve performance in every single aspect of our lives. But we need to be smart with our coffee. Here is a simple but important practice that will ensure you are in control of your caffeine intake and to make coffee work for you.

The Practice:

On a regular basis, ideally once per month, you need to take at least one week off coffee and all other sources of caffeine. Coffee is great, but long-term coffee use has a few problems. Let me first explain how caffeine actually works: We have a neurotransmitter in our brain called adenosine. Adenosine causes us to feel sleepy and builds up over the course of the day. We also have some residual adenosine in our brains when we wake up in the morning. Caffeine blocks the receptors in the brain that adenosine binds to. This means the adenosine can't bind, and therefore leads to us feeling awake. We only feel tired when the adenosine is able to bind to the receptors.

However, when caffeine binds to these receptors and doesn't allow the adenosine to bind, our brains will start to produce more receptors. This means it will take more and more caffeine to achieve the same effect. This is why your first cup of coffee after some time off always hits the hardest, but when you're having coffee every day you can have 3 espresso shots and not feel a thing.

Another consideration with having a lot of adenosine receptors is that once the caffeine wears off (caffeine has a half-life of 6 hours), the adenosine receptors become unblocked — and because we have so many receptors, a lot of adenosine can bind at once, and we experience a crash.

Fortunately, taking 7 days off each month can essentially reset these receptors and get them back to a more normal level, thus preventing these consequences.

What You Can Do:

Each month (or at least regularly) take at least 7 days completely off coffee.

I like to do it the first 7 days of each month so I always remember.

If you're like most people, you're going to experience withdrawal. So I will explain an effective method to hopefully mitigate if not completely prevent withdrawal symptoms.

Day 1: Drink one cup of coffee only (skip this day if you usually only have one cup)

Day 2: Have a cup of caffeinated tea — e.g. black or green, but no other caffeine

Day 3–7: No caffeine at all

I have found this slow ease off to be effective in managing withdrawal.

Coffee is great. But we need to be smart with it. Having high amounts of caffeine every single day is not ideal. We need to let the neurotransmitters in our brain reset.

But fortunately, by simply taking a week off each month, we can mitigate any detrimental consequences and can enjoy our coffee and all its health benefits, without any concerns."[1]

2. Green Tea

If you think your metabolism is slow, you should give green tea a try, especially Japanese matcha green tea. I used this for a week. My metabolism improved significantly but then plateaued after reaching a threshold. Still, it was helpful because my metabolism had reduced due to inactivity and trying out several dieting strategies. Green tea is also rich in polyphenols, which are natural compounds that help to reduce inflammation and fight cancer.

3. Protein

We can include protein to make us feel full and protect our muscle loss when we are on a fat loss program. We should exercise, along with the diet changes discussed in this book, to maintain our strength and muscle mass. If we have more muscle mass, most energy is taken away by these muscles and so less goes to fat stores. It is therefore recommended to include a moderate amount of strength training in our weight loss program.

Protein, too, if taken in excess (above 0.8 g protein/kg body weight/day) in adults is converted to fat and may lead to some diseases, such as hypercalciuria, and stomach, colon, rectal, pancreatic, bladder, breast, endometrial, and ovarian cancers.[2]

If we don't include a moderate level of exercise and want to lose all our fat by dieting alone, the chances are that we will get weaker and weaker day by day because 'What you don't use, you lose—that is, muscle.

I suggest short bursts of high-intensity interval training (HIIT) rather than long low-to-moderate intensity because science-backed research suggests that the former is better for the body than the latter. HIIT has been shown to improve fitness, cardiovascular health, cholesterol profiles, and insulin sensitivity, which helps stabilise blood glucose or sugar levels—of particular significance to diabetics. HIIT also reduces fat—both abdominal and the deep, visceral kind that engulfs your inner organs—while maintaining muscle mass or, in less active individuals, increasing it.[3]This is one example of why 'less' can actually be 'more' for the body in the long run.

Other suggestions for stimulating muscle growth are doing short-duration sprints in place of jogging or running for longer, and lifting heavy weights for fewer sets instead of lighter weights for more sets. Also, instead of working out 3–4 days a week, 1–2 days a week is better to give your muscles enough rest time to recover. You will realize in your next workout that, when you combine enough stimulus with enough rest, you can consistently increase your strength and muscle mass. If you have not already, I would suggest reading or listening to *Body by Science* by McGuff and Little for in-depth analysis.[4]

Vegan protein sources include beans, pulses, legumes, chickpeas, nuts, peas, vegetables, and soy chunks.

But a very high amount of protein, or whatever is more than our body can use or metabolize for energy and repair, will get stored as fat! Several of the health complications that we face today are due to over-nutrition!

So moderation, here too, is the key: eat everything in moderation.

4. Coconut oil—the fat that is a fat burner

I have included this special oil here because it is my 'go-to' healthy fat to quickly get my body into a fat-burning zone without much effort. Coconut oil contains medium-chain triglycerides (MCTs), which the body can digest quickly and convert to energy, compared with the long-chain triglycerides found in fats like olive oil. But please note that not all MCT oils are the same as coconut oil.

Our body stops complaining when we give it an alternative source of fuel that is metabolized quickly, such as coconut oil, after we reduce carbohydrates from our diet, which we need to do to trigger fat loss. I prefer wood-pressed and cold-pressed coconut oil because these are organic and less processed versions. They enhance feelings of fullness for more extended periods.

Research shows that coconut oil intake may decrease inflammation, raise levels of heart-protective high-density (HDL) cholesterol (sometimes called 'good cholesterol'), and promote insulin sensitivity.[5]

Although high in saturated fat, it has been suggested that the primary saturated fatty acid (lauric acid) in coconut oil has different metabolic and health effects compared with other saturated fatty acids such as palmitic acid, predominant in butter, palm oil, and animal fat.[6]

Millions of people worldwide struggle with stubborn abdominal fat that can be challenging to shed. Studies show that belly fat can increase the risk of many health conditions, including type 2 diabetes and heart disease. However, some ground-breaking studies have found positive effects of coconut oil on abdominal fat.

1. A 2009 study, published in *The Journal of Lipids*, consisted of testing the effects of coconut oil on a group of 40 women over 28 days.[7]The results showed that the group who ate the coconut oil had a decrease in abdominal fat. The study also found that the coconut oil showed an increase in HDL cholesterol levels.

A PubMed article talks about a study related to the medium-chain fatty acids (MCFAs) abundant in coconut fat. The results from this study indicate that medium-chain saturated oil may be more advantageous in abdominal and intermuscular fat reduction than a long-chain unsaturated oil.[8]These studies showed that diets rich in fats, such as those found in coconut oil, boosted metabolism, reduced overall caloric intake during the day, reduced body weight, and lowered body fat.

3. One study assessed body weight and fat storage relative to three different types of diets, including a low-fat diet, a high-fat diet with long chain fatty acids (LCFAs), and a high-fat diet with MCFAs. To bring about weight gain, caloric intake was adjusted for these diets.[9]

At the end of the research period (which lasted 44 days), the low-fat diet group stored an average of 0.47 g of fat per day, the LCFA group stored 0.48 g of fat per day, and the MCFA group stored only a mere 0.19 g per day (despite purposely increasing calories). Those in the MCFA group (coconut fat) had a 60% reduction in body fat stored compared to the other diets.

One fruit in particular—the coconut—is so abundant in its healing properties that it's referred to as 'the tree of life'. And, before World War II, people living in island countries, like the Philippines, consumed a diet that consisted mainly of rice, root crops, vegetables, and an abundance of that ultra-healing superfood—the coconut.

The coconut is a 'functional food,' rich in vitamins, minerals, and fiber—the essential nutritional building blocks for perfect health.

For generations, the island people considered it 'the cure for all illness' and consumed meat, milk, and coconut oil daily. Although this diet was high in saturated fat, Western conditions like diabetes, cancer, and heart disease were virtually unheard of.

Filipinos and islanders were instead rewarded with a lovely youthful complexion; soft, wrinkle-free skin; almost no skin cancer—even with excessive exposure to the year-round sun—and abundant good health.

There are nine reasons to take coconut oil daily.[10]In particular, it has been shown to protect one from viruses, bacteria, infection, cancer, thyroid problems, brain disorders, and heart problems... Plus, it beautifies our skin—and even burns fat! A saturated fat, it is chock-full of health-promoting properties and is in no way responsible for high cholesterol, obesity, heart disease, or any of the harmful effects we've been led to believe.

Finally, modern medicine and science are starting to realize this fundamental truth... and it's been a long time coming. But, sadly, not before heart disease, cancer, diabetes, obesity, and many other catastrophic diseases have reached epidemic proportions![11]

However, since there is not enough evidence to foolproof the use of high amounts of coconut oil, as with everything, I recommend using it in moderation. I take around 6 teaspoons daily, which is approximately 30 mL and has been found in studies to reduce waist size significantly if used for 4 weeks, especially in males.[12]

We can reduce the amount of fat further after we achieve our desired goal weight. It would be much better to eat a whole coconut as fresh fruit on a few days of the week, because this is a much more natural way to gain all the benefits from it.

However, I don't suggest taking anything in large quantities, even coconut oil, as in the case of the Keto diet that requires one to consume very high amounts of fat. This is not necessary to achieve our goal of fat loss. We can do this more comfortably by not worrying too much about caloric intake. We can consume various foods with complex carbs, good protein, and healthy fats with fiber salads and green leafy vegetables, along with intermittent fasting.

We should fast for an adequate number of hours to burn the excess fat between meals and also combine our fasting with moderate exercise like walking, hiking, or swimming—whatever is feasible to get into shape.

Other healthy fats are also available, such as olive oil, virgin mustard oil, and ghee or butter. Still, I have not found these as effective as coconut oil for fat-burning purposes.

We can consume coconut oil in whatever form we like, as in coffee, cooking, making recipes out of fresh coconuts, and eating fresh or dried coconuts. What is important is that we include this excellent fruit in our diets.

In the past, I tried various dieting strategies to lose weight and was successful to some extent. But, after following one for, say, a month or two, I would lose interest and it would become challenging for me to resume it.

I tried eating only vegetables with no wheat, no rice, no beans, no coconut oil, nothing. I only ate vegetables and reduced my belly fat significantly in just one month. I did it with a solid determination, forcing my body to adapt to it. I combined it with daily walking to burn extra calories. But this was not sustainable in the long run because nobody likes eating only vegetables when we have many other delicious foods to eat—right?

I have also tried fasting—no food for up to 48–72 hours—and got good results with that too, but I felt horrible: as if my body was revolting against me because I was robbing it of the nutrients that it needed to function. I lost weight, but not much belly fat, because I also had to work and could not fast for an extended period. If we can't concentrate on work and are fasting while we are supposed to be working, our performance deteriorates. We have to give the body fuel so that we don't get distracted by frequent urges to eat something.

So, after trying various strategies one after the other, I finally found a way of combining everything into this one plan, which was sustainable and did magic. And, for the first time in my life, I felt like sharing this with others like you, after figuring out what lifestyle approach was sustainable for the long term so that the weight didn't come back again if we stopped following a specific diet. The *coconut oil* had come to my rescue, and I found doing intermittent fasting and time-restricted eating to be easily manageable after adding some of this oil to my diet, which helped me switch my body to fat burning without much effort.

5. Apple cider vinegar

Consuming apple cider vinegar has been found to have many health benefits. It has also been linked to weight loss, cholesterol reduction, and blood sugar control.

Vinegar intake reduced body weight, body fat mass, and serum triglyceride levels in obese Japanese subjects.[13]

Another study found that vinegar significantly reduced blood sugar in participants who had just consumed a meal containing 50 g of carbs. It also found that the stronger the vinegar, the lower the blood sugar.[14]

Yet another study looked into the effect of vinegar on blood sugar after participants consumed carbs. It found that vinegar increased insulin sensitivity by between 19% and 34%.[15]

The addition of vinegar can also lower the glycemic index of a food, which can help reduce blood sugar spikes.[16]

However, it's essential to talk with your doctor before taking apple cider vinegar if you're already taking medications that lower blood sugar.

A study in Japan found that adding pickled foods to rice decreased the meal's glycemic index significantly.[17]

Whenever I had a simple carb-rich food without much protein and fat, I would take 1 tablespoon of apple cider vinegar mixed in 1 glass of water 30 minutes before eating. I would also walk more after taking this meal to minimize the insulin spike.

[1]https://medium.com/in-fitness-and-in-health/a-crucial-practice-for-all-coffee-drinkers-ad01ddd002fc

[2]https://www.ncbi.nlm.nih.gov/pmc/articles/PMC4045293/

[3]https://www.sciencefocus.com/the-human-body/hiit-is-changing-the-way-we-workout-heres-the-science-why-it-works/

[4]*Body by Science: A Research Based Program for Strength Training, Body Building, and Complete Fitness in 12 Minutes a Week* by Doug McGuff, MD and John Little

[5]https://www.health.harvard.edu/blog/is-there-a-place-for-coconut-oil-in-a-healthy-diet-2019011415764

[6]https://bmjopen.bmj.com/content/8/3/e020167

[7]Stanford Chiropractic Center Blog | Rethink: Why Coconut Oil KILLS Belly Fat https://www.stanfordchiropractic.com/blogs/rethink/why-coconut-oil-kills-belly-fat.html

[8]https://www.ncbi.nlm.nih.gov/pmc/articles/PMC4283167/

[9]https://www.stanfordchiropractic.com/blogs/rethink/why-coconut-oil-kills-belly-fat.html

[10]https://www.thealternativedaily.com/pages/coconutoil.php?AFFID=151114&subid=ARLinkthetruth

[11]https://www.stanfordchiropractic.com/blogs/rethink/why-coconut-oil-kills-belly-fat.html

[12]https://pubmed.ncbi.nlm.nih.gov/22164340/

[13]https://pubmed.ncbi.nlm.nih.gov/19661687/

[14]https://pubmed.ncbi.nlm.nih.gov/16015276/

[15]https://pubmed.ncbi.nlm.nih.gov/14694010/

[16]https://www.healthline.com/nutrition/blood-sugar-spikes#8.-Introduce-some-vinegar-into-your-diet

[17]https://pubmed.ncbi.nlm.nih.gov/12792658/

CHAPTER VI

Choosing the Right Kind of Fat

I have always felt that animal fat and plant fat act differently on the body, and that one may be more effective than the other for fat loss.

An article in *TIME* said that plant fat seemed to have a more significant impact on healthy living than animal fat, especially monosaturated fat.[1]

Whatever the case, I have found that food cooked in virgin mustard oil keeps me full for longer hours and also that, when I take coconut oil, I don't feel the urge to eat anything for long periods. Sometimes we have to listen to our body, make a few adjustments, try out different types of fats, and see what works best for us. There is no one-size-fits-all approach, but we can find out how we feel after having a certain kind of fat. We all now know that trans fats, found in highly processed vegetable oils, are bad for our health and we need to avoid them as much as possible.

I have tried eating peanuts and other nuts such as almonds, walnuts, cashews, and pistachios but, unless and until I take some coconut oil with or without them, I feel hungry again in just a few hours. My body doesn't switch to fat-burning mode as swiftly as desired, even when there is primarily fat in those nuts.

Whenever I take three teaspoons of coconut oil with even just plain water, it works and does its job. Then, although I may feel mild hunger following its digestion, I can avoid eating because my body uses that coconut oil and enables me to go more hours before needing to eat again.

I have gone anywhere from 9 to 14 hours with only a coffee with some coconut oil before feeling hungry and, after sleeping, have observed good weight loss the very next day. What else do I need to convince me? That's how incredible this oil is!

You can get your body into fat-burning mode quickly with the help of this special coconut oil. You don't get hunger pangs following its digestion. You won't feel dizziness, light-headedness, or lethargy when not eating anything after digesting your last meal if you had three teaspoons of coconut oil with it.

But if we force our body to switch to fat-burning with other kinds of fats that are not converted to energy by our body as swiftly as coconut oil, we don't feel good and are not motivated to continue doing it. We also have to wait for many more hours before the body starts to use these other fats.

[1]https://time.com/5208817/plant-animal-fats/

CHAPTER VII

Foods to Avoid or Minimize

I recommend avoiding or minimizing the following.

1. Highly processed so-called 'junk' foods and simple carbohydrates such as wheat and rice

I stopped consuming wheat and rice entirely and switched to millets. Although I did not feel full for longer after starting to eat millets, maybe because they were also to some degree, processed, as some millets cannot be easily digested by some of us because of their high fiber content. So one should start with small quantities and increase gradually. I did not put on any weight and I minimized my heartburn after including millets in my diet in place of wheat bread and white rice.

When I ate soy chunks cooked in mustard oil, I could go for a much longer period without eating, feeling full due to the higher amount of protein in the soy chunks, healthy virgin mustard oil, and the fiber in the onions, tomatoes, and garlic that I added. Onions are also said to act as prebiotics, so there's dual benefit. Prebiotics are non-digestible food ingredients that promote the growth of beneficial microorganisms in the intestines, hence improving our gut health. I also included white beans in my diet—these are high in protein and potassium. But this diet did not control my weight, which increased because I was eating a good amount of carbs, although a complex mix.

It was only then, when I incorporated intermittent fasting or time-restricted eating into my lifestyle, that I started to see visible results of fat loss even when eating beans, which are not allowed in a low-carb diet.

2. High quantity of sweets or sugary items such as soda

We must not regularly include large amounts of sweets or sugary items such as soda in our diet. Once in a while is okay but, if you take them daily, it will ruin your efforts to achieve weight loss.

3. Highly processed vegetable oils or so-called 'trans fats'

We should minimize or eliminate all kinds of highly processed vegetable oils or trans fats, which are detrimental if we want to achieve good health.

4. High amounts of animal fats

I do not recommend high amounts of animal fats, specifically because I do not find them beneficial to our body for fat-burning purposes.

One gram of fat equals nine calories, so it is easy to eat too many of them if we are not eating the right kinds of fats at certain times of the day, planned strategically for our advantage.

5. Table salt

While a pinch of table salt is okay, I would suggest taking more Himalayan pink salt or rock salt because these have more natural minerals and are not as harmful as table salt.

CHAPTER VIII

Hack– My Natural Special Oil

Most of us may be aware of what intermittent fasting and time-restricted eating are. They are about giving ourselves a particular time frame for eating and not eating. When we eat randomly whenever we want, our body doesn't get a good chance to tap into our fat reserves for its daily energy needs and it keeps burning the food that we last ate. Hence, it is crucial for us to give our body a good window of opportunity in which it can use our stored fat and thereby help in our fat loss.

For simplification:

- an eating window;
- a fasting window.

In the eating window, we have to eat whatever we usually eat, preferably some complex carbohydrates, protein, and healthy fats.

Then, in the fasting window, we do not eat or drink anything other than plain water to give our body a complete chance to tap into our fat reserves and use them for energy instead of food.

If you don't get enough complex carbs, protein, fiber, and healthy fat with each meal, it will be difficult for you to refrain from eating in your fasting window.

For illustration purposes, I present the following plan:

Eat 4 hours before your bedtime, sleep for 8 hours, then eat or drink anything other than water after about 4 hours of waking up. If you wake up at 7 a.m., eat your first meal at 11 a.m., and take your last meal at 7 p.m. This way, your eating window will be morning 11 a.m. to evening 7 p.m. (that is, 8 hours)and your fasting window will be evening 7 p.m. to morning 11 a.m. (that is, 16 hours).

If you feel hungry after 7 p.m. before you go to sleep, you can increase slightly the amount of fat and protein you eat, or just drink some coconut oil in plain water. If you plan to sleep at around 11 p.m., you should not drink it in coffee at this time because the caffeine will disrupt your sleep. Also, your last meal of the day should not contain many simple carbs, such as white bread or white rice, because you will get hungry before bed and end up eating something that will spoil the whole process.

You can start with any window in the 24 hours of the day from, say, 12:12 (12 hours' fasting, 12 hours' eating)—which people who are new to this kind of fasting and eating lifestyle generally start with. Then they gradually move to 14:10 (14 hours' fasting time, 10 hours' eating time), or 16:8 (16 hours' fasting time, 8 hours' eating time), or 20:4 (20 hours' fasting time, 4 hours' eating time), adding more hours of fasting when not seeing desirable benefits in a larger eating window.

Instead of eating large meals, I eat 2–3 small ones because otherwise I feel sleepy. I consume coffee with 3 teaspoons of coconut oil a couple of hours or so after each meal. This means that I don't have to worry about including fats with my meals. The coffee and coconut oil combination serves as a double-edged sword for the breakdown of fat reserves.

My main meals mainly consist of white beans. Yes, that's right! Just beans, sometimes soy chunks, sometimes chickpeas, sometimes kidney beans, according to my mood if I get bored sticking to one type of food for a long time.

I may eat some sweets, popcorn, burgers, or sandwiches, but only occasionally when I feel like eating, which is not more than twice in a given week. This does not lead to any substantial weight gain because I keep the portions small, eat them slowly, enjoy the texture, and feel good. I also make sure that I have coffee with coconut oil at least once, even on these 'cheat' days!

After my body has finished metabolizing the coconut oil, I feel mild hunger. Then, I decide not to eat because I know it is gentle and will disappear within minutes. And then the same thing happens: I feel mild heartburn as my body releases bile and prepares to burn fat as energy. This is when the magic happens to us all: our brain starts performing smoothly; our alertness peaks; our pains, if any (like lower back pain), reduce in intensity. We are more focused on the task that we are doing because there is not much feeling of hunger, only increased mental focus and clarity of thought—and we feel fuller.

The best fasting window is between stopping eating a few hours before sleep and within a few hours of waking up, which is the most natural and what most people do. However, if they are not getting their desired results, I recommend adding the *special oil*, wood-pressed or cold-pressed coconut oil, to their diet in any form possible, as well as increasing their fasting window.

Some people don't get much benefit until they fast for 20 hours, which means they have just a 4-hour window in which to eat. One coffee with coconut oil, followed by one large meal after 3–4 hours, and that's it.

Whenever you feel dizzy, light-headed, lethargic, hungry, or unwilling to continue fasting, you should immediately break your fast. You should have a light snack first and wait for some time before having any large meal, especially if you have been fasting for a long time.

Body fat burning takes place differently in women compared with men. While women can start seeing their belly fat melt within a matter of 1–2 weeks, men first lose fat from other areas of their body, like their cheeks and chest. But, eventually, after following this program consistently for a few weeks, their body will begin to reduce their belly fat.

If you have much fat to lose and are on a mainly carbohydrate-rich diet, you will see results straightaway. You can weigh yourself daily on a digital weighing machine just after waking up and you will notice a drop in weight, although some people with stubborn body fat will take more time to detect such reduction.

Just concentrate on how you feel while being on this program. Has your sleep quality improved? Has your gap between going to bed and falling asleep reduced? Are you feeling more refreshed after waking up? Are you getting fewer hunger pangs or cravings than before? Are you more alert during the day, having sustained energy mostly throughout? Things like that. These are a few indicators to tell you that you are moving in the right direction. Have some patience and you will notice the reduction in belly fat because, first, you become healthier and then you lose fat. So your concentration must be on getting healthy first and not so much on losing weight.

You can always tweak the program by varying the eating and fasting windows that suit you or keep you going for days and months to come.

What is most significant is to start with what you can do and gradually move from there to what seems more difficult for you. Then you can apply these strategies. Even progress of 1% daily will get you the results you want in a few weeks or a couple of months. Just stick to the program if you are feeling healthier than before.

I could not resist the temptation of trying out this method so I made changes to my eating and fasting windows, strictly coupled with going out in bright light as soon as I woke up and staying there for 1–2 hours, and I found the following changes to my body.

As I worked the night shift, I started with my last meal at 7 p.m. (Indian Standard Time), rather than my usually earlier time. I tended to add a couple of snacks before I went to bed in the morning, sometimes eating until 6, 7, or 8 a.m. until I felt like sleeping. My sleeping time was not fixed—7, sometimes 8, sometimes not getting to sleep even until about 11. I tried whatever I could to get to sleep in good time but tended to fail miserably at it.

Here are two of the changes I observed when applying everything discussed in this book:

1. I got canker sores, which I usually get whenever I drastically change my eating and sleeping times. They were relieved and cured quickly by using over-the-counter gels.

2. I also started waking up at a fixed time every day by setting an alarm, going out in daylight, around 3–4 p.m., and applying a night light filter on my computer and mobile 1 hour before I intended to sleep. This way, I started to feel drowsy close to my bedtime. I could hardly keep my eyes open, had to force myself to shut down my computer half an hour earlier than expected, and slept like a baby for a total of 5 hours approximately. Then, I woke up as if I had slept for 10 hours, feeling refreshed and willing to get out of bed immediately. This was just because I had reduced my eating window from 12 hours to 6 hours. My body had begun thinking that I didn't have access to much food so, by waking me up early, it was preparing me to go to bed early,

sleep tight, and then go in search of food.

This scenario was in Dr Panda's book, which I discussed in Chapter 2: the subject mice, when kept on a time-restricted eating program, woke up earlier than usual and started searching for food. So I think the same thing was happening to me.

My last meal was at 7 p.m. and I went to bed at 6 a.m. I woke up at 11 a.m., so I had 16 hours of fasting. Adding 2 more hours of fasting (until 1 p.m.) equalled 18 hours. I had my first meal at 1 p.m., coffee at 3 p.m., and supper at 7 p.m., mixing another 3 teaspoons of wood-pressed coconut oil into my food at this time.

I repeated this for 3–4 days, the same thing happened, and I lost 1 kg. I did not feel much hunger or craving in my fasting window from 7 p.m. to 1 p.m. But I was worried because I started to feel sleepy before finishing my work. I decided to tweak my plan so as to stay awake more by eating much closer to bedtime by extending my eating window—for example, first meal at 2 p.m. and last meal at 12 a.m., which gave me 10 hours of eating window and, if I sleep at 6 a.m., it's just 6 hours of fasting before I sleep rather than 11 hours of fasting before bedtime as done previously.

I wanted to stick to this routine for many reasons:

1. I felt good and noticed that my body was supporting this regime.

2. I no longer had insomnia. I fell asleep faster and woke up refreshed in a comparatively much shorter time frame. I used that time to work on my skills related to my job. I also considerably reduced my activity on social media to improve my quality of life exponentially.

3. I lost weight, which was motivating.

4. I employed everything I had learned from different resources and study, and from my own experience and understanding. I got a near-complete picture as to how I could lose weight comfortably, sleep tight, time my sleep–wake cycle correctly, and feel energetic throughout my day!

After trying this for some time and noticing positive changes like never before, I was very excited about my results. I felt so motivated and confident that I asked my wife to do the same. She was suffering from pain and swelling in her legs down from the knees, above the ankles, and could not lose weight. I linked this to non-alcoholic fatty liver disease, because she said that her liver had been weak from her childhood. Now she was getting more symptoms due to this.

Here are the changes that I made to my wife's diet and lifestyle, and the results she achieved:

1. At first, I restricted the eating window to between 7 a.m. and 4 p.m. to check if this would work for her. I told her to eat mainly peanuts, pistachios, and some salads, and to reduce the number of simple carbs like white bread (roti or chapatti) and rice from her diet, replacing these with the nuts. I also told her to have Halim seeds (1 teaspoon after soaking them for a couple of hours) taken with milk in between the 2 meals that she was having. This was because she used to have an iron deficiency, loss of hair, etc. I came to know this tip from a famous Indian nutritionist, Rujuta Diwekar, because she recommended it to women to help them avoid gender-related health complications.

But, because my wife was not used to a carb-restricting diet, she felt dizzy in the evening, lazy, and not willing to continue the program. However, I advised her to stay on it because I was so confident that it would help her.

2. I gave my wife a pair of compression stockings to wear and suggested walking daily; continuing with the program; and, instead of having a carb-rich meal in the evening, eating soy chunks cooked with virgin mustard oil and spices. She somehow kept to this regimen for 1 more day but didn't much like the taste of soy chunks.

So I changed my wife's evening meal from soy chunks to white beans because I knew these had a number of complex carbs, B-vitamins, and good protein, and also tasted better than soy chunks. My idea was to avoid her taking any carb-rich food devoid of protein and fat as her last meal before bed.

This worked and she was more motivated to continue with the program. I also found that she felt hungry in the evening before bed and did not feel like walking, which I had recommended, because she was not taking coconut oil as I had suggested.

So I moved my wife's eating window, from morning 7 a.m. to 4 p.m. afternoon, to 4 hours later—from morning 11 a.m. to evening 7 p.m. She had to stop having her morning tea because of this. I told her that, if she were feeling hungry and did not want to take coconut oil because she did not like its taste, beans with virgin mustard oil would be a good help; and also that, because she would be eating closer to bedtime, she would be able to sleep before she would feel hungry again. This plan worked for the evening but not for the morning.

3. My wife used to drink tea every morning. After its discontinuation, she got caffeine withdrawal symptoms, which gave her headaches for the next 2–3 days, but nonetheless she stopped it entirely by willpower. I explained that, because she was feeling hungry in the evening and not much in the morning after waking up,

we could bank on this and I told her to continue without food or tea until she felt like eating. Doing so would also maintain her 18:6 intermittent fasting window. That would keep her body in the fat-burning zone even after waking up until she ate something. I also told her that her headaches would go away in a few days.

And this is what happened—my wife started losing inches from the waist and she was not getting any more headaches after stopping her tea in the morning. Now she was fully motivated and willing to continue with interest and commitment because she could see the results.

Moreover, the pain and swelling in her feet also started to reduce by about 10 days into this regime. She lost a total of 5 kg weight in just 3 weeks, mostly from her waist. She eradicated most of her leg swelling and pain after strictly adhering to my suggestions for 30 days. Her metabolism also improved, she felt better, and the swelling and pain in her legs went completely after about 6 weeks into this program.

So you can see how we have to make some changes according to personal choice, lifestyle, and preferences, but still get the desired results because of time-restricted eating and fasting with a few diet modifications and moderate exercise or brisk walking.

There are a few other points to note when on this program:

1. Never feel guilty or bad about eating any food that makes you happy or that your body is craving after following this diet for a few days. This can be used to your advantage.

You will be more motivated to continue with your diet and lifestyle modifications if you manage to eat and drink in moderation the foods that you love—that you crave—say, a couple of times a week. This will not result in any weight gain and it may boost your mood. This is because food is not just a source of calories: people are emotionally connected to certain types of foods and, when asked to follow a strict diet, almost everybody fails. Also, if we succeed in following a strict diet for some time, we are more than likely to revert to our previous regime (assuming it was flexible enough) once we stop following the new one, although the reason for this is unclear.

After the first week into the program, my wife said she felt like eating some sweet dessert and one evening she craved it. She asked if she could eat it. She was concerned as to whether it would affect the gains she had made from the hard work of the past week. I told her to just go ahead, eat it, and feel good—not guilty—about it. And she did. The next day, she weighed herself again before taking her first meal and, to her surprise, she had lost yet another 300 g of weight, even after eating that one-off sweet dessert treat.

This is how the program should work. Feel free for a couple of cheats along the way here and there. Just come back to the fat loss plan as soon as possible. If you follow this type of strategic program, you can reward yourself with almost any food you crave a couple of times a week: it will not lead to any noticeable weight gain. Eat a small portion of it, slowly and mindfully, enjoying the texture. This will not ruin your results overall. You are not on a dieting plan: you are just strategically planning your meals in a given window and choosing not to eat in the remaining window so that your body can tap into your fat reserves to lose weight effortlessly.

2. When we keep an appropriate gap between our last meal of the day and sleep, so long as we do not eat anything close to the sleep time, our body starts to tap into our

body fat before we go to sleep. And our brain function also improves to a much greater extent when we keep a large gap between our last meal/dinner and sleep. Then, if we do not feel like eating after we wake up, we can continue our fast until lunch because the body is already in the fat-burning zone from the night before and, by doing this, we just give it more time to burn fat. So this helps in overall fat loss.

3. I generally start early by having breakfast within 1 hour of waking up. I also keep a large gap (6–8 hours) between dinner and bedtime because:

- I sleep soundly when doing so; and
- I get up swiftly in the morning because I feel very refreshed.

CHAPTER IX

Managing Stress and Anxiety

This chapter is concerned with reducing prolonged sitting-related lower back pain, which is often related to stress and anxiety.

Possible contributing factors for back pain are as follows:

1. Poor sitting posture.

2. Not changing position from sitting to moving, or walking or standing, and vice versa, every 30 minutes.

3. Stress.

4. Anxiety.

5. Depression.

6. Poor sleep.

7. Poor diet.

8. Substance addiction.

9. Post-traumatic stress disorder.

10. Unclear diagnosis.

We now know that persistent back pain is more complicated than 'weak core = back pain', Dr Caleb Burgess.[1]

We can reduce work-related back pain by proper sitting posture. We should use an ergonomic office chair, sitting up straight, mildly resting on the lumbar support. We should rest our arms on the armrest so that the weight is taken off our shoulders. We should keep our computer screens to eye level, ranging plus or minus 30 degrees up or down, and keeping the monitor at arm's length. We can use wrist pads if typing a lot. We should keep our feet firmly on the ground at around 90 degrees or so. We can check if we have about a fist-width gap between our calves and the outer edge of our chair for proper blood circulation.

Lower back pain also occurs due to the accumulation of toxins caused by a sedentary lifestyle, overuse of the spine muscles, lack of exercise, etc.

Getting out of the chair every half an hour and doing some stretching and movement, like walking, jumping jacks, or skipping (1–2 minutes), is recommended to minimize prolonged sitting-related back pain.

Simple walking for at least 30 minutes a day can reduce back pain because it delivers the essential nutrients to tackle the inflammation and stiffness in the spine by improving blood circulation in that area. Walking for 30–45 minutes daily for 1–2 weeks has been found to relieve lower back pain. I tried it, and it was extremely helpful.

I have observed that moving around in fresh air and taking slow deep breaths through the nose whenever I have the time also reduce the negative emotions associated with such lower back pain because they increase our overall serotonin levels.

We can put acupressure mats beneath our back while lying down and for as long as tolerated. Doing this can reduce pain and inflammation in our lower back because it increases blood flow to the affected region and delivers essential nutrients. I have tried this, too, and it has certainly helped to some extent.

One can also do some exercises like the 'Superman' ones to strengthen the lower back, starting with a couple of sets, which also build good mind–muscle connections, make the muscles around the spine more robust, and generally help minimize any lower back pain.

Also associated with lower back pain are anxiety, stress (such as overexposure to social media sites), depression and worry, all of which can exacerbate pain in this area for reasons not clearly understood.

One should minimize the use of social media platforms unless necessary for professional reasons. The number of likes to our posts on Facebook, positive comments, etc. raise dopamine levels in our brain, sending reward signals and feelings of happiness. But the dose should be well-controlled. If we get too many likes, or love and care reactions, our dopamine levels can rise to unhealthy levels, creating manic episodes. Don't be surprised if any article or research study confirms this.

Conversely, when we don't get expected likes or comments on our posts, we can feel depressed, especially if others are getting more. This can leaves us feeling helpless and hopeless, and the brain can't figure out what's happening.

Suppose we are getting ready to sleep and suddenly we feel like posting something on social media, say Facebook. Now we won't rest until we see some likes on our posts, which will make us feel good, and, if somebody reacts with a ha-ha reaction, we also share that ha-ha. And this is all at bedtime when our body is trying to prepare us for sleep.

Similarly, when we are awake, we find that we keep checking our mobile phones to see whether any new likes, comments, or reactions have come, and, if not, why not? Receiving these sends different signals to the brain, making us feel delighted because we like it. Otherwise, we may become depressed. These reactions occur daily and some people use such social media platforms for many hours every day. We can just imagine what they may be going through!

We need to stop this habit, especially when close to bedtime. I avoid Facebook. I use Instagram and WhatsApp, mainly because Instagram does not have the reactions feature, but I use them sparingly. I have also stopped unwanted notifications from these apps in order to focus on my more meaningful work.

I have uninstalled both Facebook and Messenger, at least from my mobile, so I'm no longer checking them regularly.

Poor sleep quality is also somehow linked to exacerbated lower back pain. I found that the intensity of my pain increased on days when I was not getting enough sleep.

[1]https://original.newsbreak.com/@david-liira-1587584/2377850876970-a-strong-core-doesn-t-always-equal-no-back-pain

CHAPTER X

Importance of Vitamin D and its Cofactors

This chapter looks into the little-known factors associated with poor vision. A couple of years ago, I read a book[1]on Kindle by Jeff T. Bowles about Vitamin D, its importance and why high doses of it are good for us because, these days, we are not exposed to as much sunlight as we used to be. Also, we cannot get much Vitamin D through diet if we have any diseases linked to its deficiency.

So I decided to take Vitamin D in supplement form (tablets), along with its cofactors mentioned in the book, without which it may act against us. I took Vitamin D3 at 7,000 IU once a day, Vitamin K2 at 100 mcg (MK-7) once a day, and magnesium, beta carotene, calcium, and zinc 1 hour after my first meal of the day.

Although I took these supplements to see if low Vitamin D might have contributed to my weight gain, I could not find any noticeable difference in my weight as a result. Nor had I had any symptoms of low Vitamin D levels earlier. I just took the supplements for experimental purposes, checking how I felt after doing so for a while.

To my surprise, I noticed something unusual, never found anywhere else—that is, changes in my vision: from not being able to clearly see the fonts on my desktop while sitting on my chair working, or the subtitles of a movie on my TV when watching from a distance of, say, 8 feet or so, without my spectacles, I could see them clearly after using these supplements for about 2.5–3 months with naked eyes. I threw my specs away because I didn't need them anymore and I was very happy that I had discovered something new. In his book, Jeff Bowles states that he took almost 100 times the recommended Vitamin D doses daily and got rid of most of his chronic diseases, which he had been unable to do with any other medical help.

Then I stopped these supplements and, after about 1 month or so, I again developed the same blurring of my vision, especially in terms of the subtitles I mentioned. But I can still see the desktop fonts today, even after stopping the supplements.

A PubMed Central article reported a study's findings that a high level of outdoor time was significantly associated with a reduced risk of incident myopia.[2]

Vitamin D3 ensures that calcium is absorbed easily and K2 (MK-7) activates the protein, osteocalcin, which integrates calcium into bone. Without D3 and K2, calcium cannot do its job effectively. Vitamin K2 (MK-7) activates the matrix GLA protein (MGP) to bind excess calcium, and promote arterial flow and flexibility.[3]So, we should take Vitamin D3 in combination with its cofactors such as Vitamin K2 (MK-7), its superior form.

Back in the olden days when people stayed outside in daylight, they used to get much higher Vitamin D from sun exposure, but these days we don't get that much. Therefore, we are prone to some diseases due to lack of this sunshine vitamin, which actually acts like a hormone, performing thousands of body functions, such as regulating the absorption of calcium and phosphorus; helping maintain normal immune function, proper growth and development of bones and teeth; and enhancing overall cardiovascular health. It also helps in reducing depression and achieving weight-loss goals.[4]

According to an article published in *The Times of India*[5], 70%–90% of Indians are deficient in Vitamin D. It's therefore essential to get enough sun to maintain optimal Vitamin D levels (unless we take supplements). Low Vitamin D levels lower your immunity and are linked with various health conditions, including osteoporosis, cancer, depression, and muscle weakness—and even death.

There are only a few foods with a significant amount of Vitamin D. These includes cod liver oil, swordfish, salmon, canned tuna, beef liver, egg yolks, and sardines. To get enough Vitamin D, one needs to eat some of these foods daily. If your diet does not give you enough Vitamin D, it is recommended to take Vitamin D supplements and to get some sun to maintain the optimal levels in the body.

Being exposed to the sun is the most natural way to get Vitamin D. The best time to sunbathe to get maximum Vitamin D is between 10 a.m. and 3 p.m. This time is also considered the safest for being exposed to the sun. However, not everyone is the same, and an article from cancer.orgadvises people to take precautions and not to expose themselves to peak direct sunlight from mid-morning to late afternoon to reduce the risk of developing skin cancer.[6]

Expose your arms, legs, back, and abdomen to get Vitamin D. Do not forget to expose your back because this allows your body to produce the maximum Vitamin D.[7]

You can choose whether or not to wear a tank top and shorts. You must wear a hat and sunglasses to protect your face and eyes.

How long should you spend in the sun to get enough Vitamin D? According to the Vitamin D Council in California, people with light-color skin need around 15 minutes while people with dark-color skin might need an hour or more. This also makes people with dark skin color more prone to be deficient in Vitamin D.

We use sunscreen to protect our skin against skin cancer and sunburn. Sunscreen has chemicals that either reflect, absorb, or scatter sunlight. When this happens, the skin is exposed to lower levels of harmful type B ultraviolet (UVB) rays.

However, UVB rays are essential for making Vitamin D, and sunscreen can stop the skin from producing Vitamin D. Studies show that sunscreen with SPF 15 or higher reduces Vitamin D3 production in the body by 99%.[8]So, if you are wearing sunscreen, you might have to spend long hours in the sunlight for your skin to produce enough Vitamin D.

Although sunlight is an excellent source of Vitamin D, too much exposure has its own health risks. Here are some possible consequences of being exposed to too much sunlight:

- Sunburn: This is one of the most common side effects of too much sunlight. Symptoms of sunburn include redness, swelling, pain, tenderness, and blisters on the skin.

- Eye damage: Too much exposure to UVB rays can damage the retina, increasing the risk of cataracts.

- Aging skin: Spending too much time in the sun can cause your skin to age faster. Some people develop wrinkles and their skin becomes loose and leathery.

- Heatstroke (also called 'sunstroke'): This is a condition in which the body's core temperature rises due to too much exposure to the sun.

- Skin cancer: Too much UVB light is a major cause of types of skin cancer.

Conclusion

Regular exposure to the sun is the most natural way to get enough Vitamin D. But do not overexpose yourself and wear sunglasses to avoid eye damage.

If your profession requires you to be in the sun for several hours, apply sunscreen.

Along with Vitamin D3 and Vitamin K2 (MK-7), I also take additional magnesium, calcium, zinc, and beta carotene when I'm on these supplements, as it was mentioned in the book I described above, to take these co-factors along with high Vitamin D3 and K2.

For magnesium, I take cacao nibs, and sweet potatoes, pumpkin, carrots, amla (Indian gooseberry) for beta carotene/vitamin A.

Readers are advised to exercise full caution before taking any supplements mentioned in this book as all are not the same and some may develop some reactions to certain foods or supplements if they do not do their own research before taking them.

[1]https://www.amazon.in/dp/B005FCKN2S/ref=dp-kindle-redirect?_encoding=UTF8&btkr=1

[2]https://www.ncbi.nlm.nih.gov/pmc/articles/PMC5599950/

[3]https://betteryou.com/pages/vitamin-d-and-vitamin-k

[4]https://onlinelibrary.wiley.com/doi/full/10.1111/j.1365-2796.2008.02008.x

[5]'The Right Way to Get Vitamin D from the Sun', *The Times of India.* https://m.timesofindia.com/life-style/health-fitness/health-news/the-right-way-to-get-vitamin-d-from-the-sun/photostory/77370069.cms

[6]https://www.cancer.gov/about-cancer/causes-prevention/risk/sunlight

[7]https://www.medicalnewstoday.com/articles/326167#boosting-vitamin-d

[8]https://www.medicalnewstoday.com/articles/317278#Sunscreen-may-reduce-vitamin-D-3-production-by-99-percent

CHAPTER XI

Why Do We Get Cravings?

This chapter discusses cravings, ways to reduce them, and how and when to eat what we want and still lose weight.

Eating junk foods, simple carbohydrates, and sweets that lead to insulin spikes, and are generally devoid of vital nutrients, lead to our craving more of these types of foods—and in a matter of only a couple of hours.

Cravings will automatically go away once you have properly educated yourself about why you are getting them. When you include healthy fats like coconut oil in your diet, your body has an easy fuel source other than carbs to switch to when it has finished digesting your last meal. It can then tap into the fat deposits and use them for energy. Also, suppose you eat a mix of complex carbs, a good amount of protein, healthy fats, and fiber or salads or vegetables. After this type of meal or snack, you feel fuller with comparatively lower insulin spikes and fewer cravings.

Also, whenever you feel like eating any of the restricted items on this program, you are welcome to eat them so long as you reduce the portion and frequency. Just eat them at the right time and in small quantities so that you do not spoil your efforts so far.

Listen to your body. If you don't feel like eating something, you shouldn't. Wait for the hunger to kick in, drink plain water and see if the craving disappears. It will go away if it is mild. Feel free to eat when you feel like doing so within your eating window, or even outside your eating window, if you find out that something is not working right. Investigate and fix it before trying again.

I learned that most Japanese people eat only two meals a day and stop eating when they notice that they are 80% full. They follow this intermittent fasting, live a long life, and are also generally slim. You can read or listen to a book called *IKIGAI: The Japanese Secret to a Long and Happy Life* if you ever want to dig deeper into what they do for longevity and optimal weight.[1]

Enjoy breaking all the rules discussed in this book when on a vacation or at a party. Just keep in mind that you should return to this fat loss plan as soon as possible. And I know that you will come back to it because you will feel so good both mentally and physically that you will be more motivated than ever after embarking on this journey towards achieving optimum health.

I deliberately did not call this flexible fat loss plan a 'dieting plan' because it is not—it is a lifestyle!

Last but not least, I forgot to mention that—before your body switches to fat-burning mode—you will feel a little hunger, or as though your stomach is empty. You should just ignore this and, within minutes, you will feel some heartburn—indicating that your body has switched into fat burning. When this happens, we don't feel hungry anymore, and we can continue with our work and eat only when we have an increased feeling of hunger.

The people who were not achieving any fat loss while following the 12:12 hours of the eating–fasting window got results when they switched to 10:14—that is, 10 hours of eating, 14 of fasting. I got my results when I switched to the 8:16 window—that is, 8 hours of eating, 16 of fasting. I observed maximum fat loss when following the 4:20 window: 4 hours of eating, 20 of fasting. We can reverse insulin resistance to a large extent if we practice intermittent fasting, as suggested by Dr Eric Berg.[2]

I recommend fasting under the supervision of your doctor if you want to get help with insulin resistance, as is the case with diabetes. If we are taking some glucose-lowering medicines and following this regime, our glucose level may come down naturally and the doses of these medications would need to be adjusted. We wouldn't be able to do this without the help of a doctor. So always feel free to reach out to registered dieticians and doctors, and let them know that you want to follow this kind of program and to be monitored by them to do so more effectively.

[1]https://www.amazon.in/Ikigai-H%C3%A9ctor-Garc%C3%ADa/dp/178633089X

[2]https://www.youtube.com/watch?v=PQWDBd2wASg

Final Words: Conclusion And Recap

It's necessary to give the body some window in which to burn the stored fat around our belly because that's what it is expected to do.

To achieve this, we must keep the fasting window around our sleeping schedule so that we minimize its effect, if any, on our work time when we are more concerned about productivity than anything else. And this is in tune with nature too, because we have day and night for this exact purpose: to eat between sunrise and sunset, not from sundown to morning.

Our internal clock also functions according to this day and night cycle. Many years ago, when we did not have light or work during nighttime, and more sunlight, daylight, fresh air, movement, and activity in the daytime, we did not have to worry much about what and how we were eating. Now, since we have access to food 24/7 and to work during the night, we have to stick to a different routine that will serve our purpose.

The most important points to keep in mind, again, are as follows.

1. Getting enough sleep is crucial to our overall health.

2. Fixing our circadian rhythm: go out in broad daylight after waking up, preferably before 4 p.m. (in case you work night shifts like me) so that we can trigger all the necessary chemical reactions inside our body, signaling that our day has started. Our body will take care of the rest, like preparing us to sleep at the end of the day.

3. Sticking to some bed and waking-up time rituals can help the body prepare for the sleep–wake cycle to some extent.

4. Not eating close to bedtime can have a positive impact on sleep quality and the amount of fat we lose. This is because maximum fat loss and repair take place when our body is in a fat-burning zone before bedtime and then when we sleep.

5. Practicing intermittent fasting or time-restricted eating with the help of healthy fats such as coconut oil can take our body into the fat-burning zone without much effort. These oils are easy to convert into energy when required by our body, so the body doesn't complain much when we reduce our carb intake.

6. Recognizing that strong cravings for simple carbs or junk food come because of our poor food choices and lack of high-quality sleep, and that they reduce when we provide the correct types of nutrient required by the body and in a given time frame because we also want to maintain our optimal body weight.

7. Getting our body to switch to a fat-burning mode not only helps us to lose excess weight but also to achieve enhanced mental focus, clarity, and alertness. Any pain minimizes and our sleep quality improves because there's a more efficient fuel that our brain likes to use—ketones, which are produced when our body starts burning fat as fuel instead of carbs.

8. Getting an adequate amount of Vitamin D and its cofactors leads to better health. Its deficiency has been linked to many diseases and conditions, including osteoporosis, cancer, depression, and muscle weakness.

9. Adding some natural forms of exercise to our fat loss regimen is required so that we do not feel weak while on this program. Anything from a few push-ups to Superman exercises to jumping jacks, to mountain climbing to hiking, or even simple outdoor walking can be very beneficial for

health if done regularly.

10. Taking frequent breaks in the daytime and increasing our movement when we are not working out can have a positive impact on our overall health.

11. Limiting our use of social media sites like Facebook can have a similarly positive impact on our mental health. It may increase our focus on our work if we turn deaf ears to these addictive websites that may cause mania. One must use such sites sparingly.

12. Including a good amount of healthy fats is essential, especially if we are trying to lose weight, because not doing so may lead to gallstones. Eating healthy fats helps your gallbladder contract and empty on a regular basis. Obesity can also lead to gallstones because it "alters the balance of cholesterol versus lecithin versus bile acids in the gallbladder," says William Silverman, MD, Professor of Medicine in the Division of Gastroenterology and Hepatology at the University of Iowa Hospitals and Clinics.[1]Excess body weight also makes it more difficult for the gallbladder to empty and this allows cholesterol-rich bile to accumulate and harden into stones. Losing excess weight helps minimize your risk of gallstones. Slow, steady weight loss is preferable to crash diets, and this is especially important when it comes to gallstones. Rapid weight loss, say 3 or more pounds per week, can trigger gallstones for the same reasons as obesity because it alters the balance of cholesterol, lecithin, and bile acids, and prevents the gallbladder from emptying adequately.

13. Eating foods not suggested in this program occasionally does not lead to much weight gain. I always feel free to reward myself with them in moderate amounts a couple of times a week when I fancy them after following this regimen for a few days. But when I see the results of

my losing weight almost effortlessly, I'm always motivated to continue following this ultimate fat loss plan most days of the week.

14. Keeping a log of our daily food intake, amount and type, our eating and fasting window hours, our sleep–wake timings, our weight, how we feel, etc., can give us a better picture of where we are heading. We can tweak this program here and there, see what works best for us and what's feasible, because everyone is different.

With this kind of lifestyle, we can save time because we will get enough sleep in a comparatively shorter amount of time than previously. We will also save time spent in cooking and eating, and also money when we choose not to eat in a particular fasting window—as well as achieving general health and well-being. We can use that time and money saved for other purposes, like learning new skills, or doing a side hustle and earning more. So it's a kind of a win–win situation for everybody, even if someone doesn't intend to lose weight and is more inclined towards just maintaining it.

I have tried to put together whatever I have learned and applied in my own life because I have seen results that promote general good health and well-being by maintaining a healthy weight and minimizing stress—even increasing work production because we get healthier and are more inclined to work as we feel more energetic.

Once again, I would like to thank you for taking some time to read this book. I hope I have been of some help to you in your journey towards achieving better health and wisdom!

Pradeep Kumar Pandey
Instagram: er.pradeep.pandey
e-mail: healthfrat@gmail.com

[1]https://www.everydayhealth.com/gallbladder/symptoms/link-between-gallstones-obesity-weight-loss/

About The Author

Pradeep Kumar Pandey is a Bachelor of Engineering graduate and works as a medical transcriptionist. He completed his Diploma in Health, Nutrition, and Weight Loss because he was interested in pursuing a deeper understanding of modern diet- and lifestyle-related health concerns and solutions. A resident of Indore (India), Pradeep has read hundreds of books related to health and fitness, and he has resolved his own health issues such as stubborn belly fat, insomnia, and sleep disorder.

Pradeep decided to write this book when he found sustainable and conclusive approaches to achieving optimum health by weight loss and improvement in sleep. He has been experimenting with various diets and weight-loss strategies, and has gained considerable experience from them. He now wants to share his success and learning with his readers.

When not working or writing, Pradeep spends his time playing chess, hiking in the mountains, learning about business analytics, and studying strategic charts for trading and investing in stock markets.

Weight Loss—A Sustainable Approach: Lose Excess Fat this Vegan Way and Sleep like a Baby is Pradeep's first book.